D1623978

happy birthday . . . blah, blah, blah

happy birthday . . . blah, blah, blah

tim and phyllis

MikWright, Ltd.

**Andrews McMeel
Publishing**

Kansas City

we respectfully dedicate this book to the she-bully that fought phyllis in the ninth grade and to the boys who taunted tim on bus route six.

we harbor no ill feelings.

ISBN 0-7407-0492-3

www.mikwright.com

03 RDS 10 9 8

Library of Congress Catalog Card Number: 99-66186

acknowledgments

happy birthday . . . blah, blah, blah is a compilation of tim and phyllis's loaded greeting card line, which evolved from family photographs and contributions from their slightly skewed firends. *happy birthday . . . blah, blah, blah* says very little about the human condition except that we're human . . . goofy one minute and ridiculous the next.

the following list acknowledges those who believed in us from ground zero.

to shawn: thanks for teaching us that printing is not an exact science.

to gatito tigre: you're the best condo cat ever!

to our brothers and sisters: we asked mom and no, we're not adopted.

to grady: pa-pa, pa-pa, pa-pa, pa-pa. pease. pease. pease. pease. thanks for go-fering as needed (nice jeep).

to our airline friends: what do you mean canceled? can i get an upgrade?

happy birthday! come on in!

i'm sorry, but robert's got diarrhea and the kids
both have lice, so . . .
it's just going to be us.

i hope you're hungry!

timmy was only too happy to play the mommy.

so i had this great idea to
get you a stripper for your birthday,
but mother was booked.

happy birthday.

in retrospect,
earl should have married his
other cousin.

come on kitten!

we've never done it in a cathedral.

oh, for god's sake edgar, roll down the window!

happy birthday.

now that i've got old lady kravitz's
house set on fire, it should be
about three minutes before those
big, strong firemen arrive.
do I look alright?

nadine . . . that wig looks fabulous!
but, how does it work on linoleum?

happy birthday.

let me down martin!

i'm losing my grip on your back hair!

every year he would try out and
every year he would get cut.
finally he gave up cheerleading
and signed up for baseball.

perhaps there was some truth to
dorothy's alien abduction story.

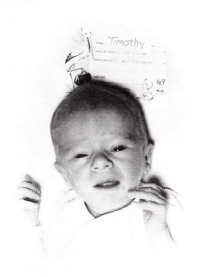

you don't have to yell!
obviously i can hear you.

happy birthday.

there could be worse things than having
another birthday.

you're kidding! i get both nipples?

doll, for your birthday i have some valuable
advice. never use a store brand cream of
mushroom soup and never let 'em know
you faked it.

i couldn't give a shit if i tried.

pardon me . . . just a little advice;

a shake for breakfast
a shake for lunch
and a sensible dinner.

happy birthday.

you know i'm not wearing any underwear.

cecil! you didn't use protection?

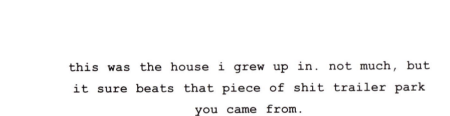

this was the house i grew up in. not much, but it sure beats that piece of shit trailer park you came from.

some say that people look and even act like their pets. well, now i can tell you that if vivian lifts her leg . . . i'm gonna lose it.

happy birthday.

now that's enough boys!
we've got flowers to arrange.

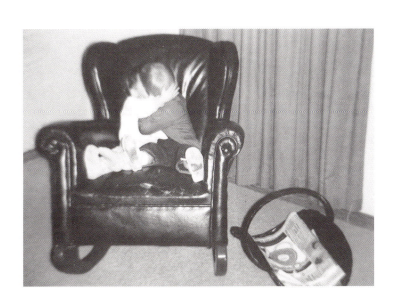

well, at least for now,
we know where your mother's
rash isn't.

our next contestant
in the swimsuit competition
is mr. tennessee; herb odum.
herb enjoys hand puppets,
water aerobics, rabbit hunting,
and cross-stitch.
herb was also voted this year's
mr. congeniality.

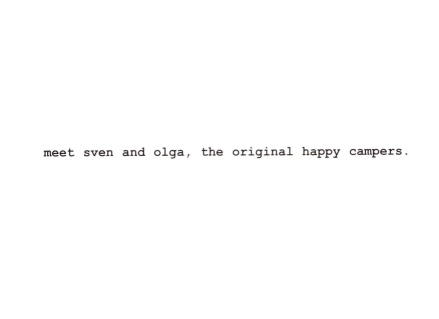

meet sven and olga, the original happy campers.

george always seemed to have a lot in common
with the ladies. often he would stop by
dottie's to gossip over brunch. then it was
straight back to the machine shop.
isn't that queer?

happy birthday.

like a divining rod, cliffy's hair could spot
a plane anywhere.

hi. my name is kevin. i am sad. my kitten is
gone. mommy said he ran away. but, i think
that's a bunch of shit and he got shot by
that bastard next door.

feeling a little anal?

you may see a man with two mules.

i see three jackasses.

mabel!

are you teaching that boy to cook?

what next . . . interpretive dance?

happy birthday to you,

(you were a mistake)

happy birthday to you,

(the condom broke)

happy birthday mary beth,

(we can't afford to keep you)

happy birthday to you.

your mother looks good, but
your father looks better.

not now mom, i'm a wreck. i've got a cake in
the oven, i'm supposed to meet sidney at the
ballet by eight, and i still haven't packed
for key west. now, for the last time mother . . .
i still don't have a girlfriend.

they tell me i used to lay in bed with
father's amputated arm to get me to go to
sleep. wasn't that sweet?

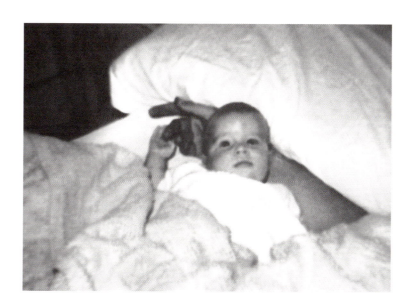

and just then jesus appeared and said . . .
"hey, kid, it's my birthday and that's
my puppy!"

it was all about timothy and his carousel cake—
the perfect prelude to his future stage name . . .
"mary a go-go round."

about the authors

tim mikkelsen is a transplanted minnesotan now living in charlotte, north carolina. after years in the airline industry, tim now writes and enjoys an occasional vodka tonic. phyllis wright-herman, also a retired airline customer service representative, resides near charlotte with her husband and daughter. phyllis is a coffee critic and the vibrance behind MikWright.

friends for fifteen years, tim and phyllis never lose sight of the role that humor plays in their lives.

triplett-hardman photography   charlotte, nc